WHITE-TAILED DEER

by Katie Marsico

Children's Press®

An Imprint of Scholastic Inc.
New York Toronto London Auckland Sydney
Mexico City New Delhi Hong Kong
Danbury, Connecticut

Content Consultant
Dr. Stephen S. Ditchkoff
Professor of Wildlife Sciences
Auburn University
Auburn, Alabama

Photographs © 2014: Alamy Images/Gregory/Photri Images: 7; Bob Italiano: 44 foreground, 45 foreground; Dreamstime: 2 background, 3, 44 background, 45 background (Ivan Chuyev), 1, 46 (Mike Rogal), 31 (Steven Oehlenschlager), cover (Tony Campbell); Getty Images/ Tom Edwards/Visuals Unlimited: 19; Media Bakery: 2 inset, 12 (James Urbach), 20 (Paul E Tessier); Minden Pictures/Rob Tilley: 23; Shutterstock, Inc./visceralimage: 4, 5 background, 35; Superstock, Inc.: 16 (Animals Animals), 5 top, 11 (imagebroker.net), 8, 15, 24, 27, 28 (Minden Pictures), 36 (Terry A Parker/All Canada Photos); The Granger Collection/Theodor de Bry/Jacques Le Moyne de Morgues: 32; The Image Works: 40 (Larry Mulvehill), 5 bottom, 39 (Tom Bushey).

Library of Congress Cataloging-in-Publication Data
Marsico, Katie, 1980– author.
White-tailed deer / by Katie Marsico.
pages cm. — (Nature's children)
Summary: "This book details the life and habits of white-tailed deer."—Provided by publisher.
Audience: 9–12.
Audience: Grades 4 to 6.
ISBN 978-0-531-21230-1 (lib. bdg.) – ISBN 978-0-531-25440-0 (pbk.)
1. White-tailed deer—Juvenile literature. 2. White-tailed deer—Behavior—Juvenile literature. I. Title. II. Series: Nature's children (New York, N.Y.)
QL737.U55M2967 2014
599.65'2—dc23   2013021638

Printed in China 62
SCHOLASTIC, CHILDREN'S PRESS, and associated logos are trademarks and/or registered trademarks of Scholastic Inc.

1 2 3 4 5 6 7 8 9 10 R 23 22 21 20 19 18 17 16 15 14

White-Tailed Deer

Class; Subclass	Mammalia; Theria
Order	Artiodactyla
Family; Subfamily	Cervidae; Capreolinae
Genus	*Odocoileus*
Species	*Odocoileus virginianus*
World distribution	Native to North, Central, and South America; introduced to other continents, including Europe and Australia
Habitats	Environments that feature thickets, including fields, meadows, and forests; also found in farmlands, deserts, and swamps
Distinctive physical characteristics	Males have antlers that reach up to 30 inches (76 centimeters) in length and feature a series of sharp points called tines; average weight of 70 to 300 pounds (32 to 136 kilograms); average length of 4.6 to 5.6 feet (1.4 to 1.7 meters); eyes on the sides of the head; large, cupped ears that move in different directions; long, slender body; muscular legs that end in narrow hooves; reddish-brown coat with a white underside in summer; coat fades to grayish-brown in winter; short tail that is covered in white fur on its underside
Habits	Communicates by grunting, releasing scents, and snorting; relies on speed and agility to escape predators; uses hooves and antlers for self-defense
Diet	Feeds mainly on buds, leaves, shoots, lichens, bark, berries, fruits, grains, nuts, and mushrooms

WHITE-TAILED DEER

Contents

CHAPTER 1

Mealtime in the Meadow

The early morning sun rises over a lush green meadow in the southeastern United States. Bumblebees begin to lazily buzz among the wildflowers. A stream trickles in the distance. A white-tailed deer does not interrupt the calm and quiet of this summer scene. Instead, the reddish-brown doe silently nibbles on the leaves and weeds that surround her.

Every so often, she raises her head from her meal to make sure no predators are approaching. She also must look out for her spotted fawn. The baby is lying still in the brush nearby, where the doe has hidden it.

White-tailed deer are the smallest species of North American deer. These hoofed, plant-eating mammals are found throughout North, Central, and South America. People have also introduced small populations of white-tailed deer to other continents, including Europe and Australia.

White-tailed deer are a common sight in the grassy fields and meadows of North America.

A Closer Look at Common Habitats

White-tailed deer are found throughout a wide variety of habitats. In North America, they generally prefer to forage in fields and meadows in the warmer months. During these times, they seek shade amid groups of broad-leaved and coniferous— or cone-bearing—trees. In cold weather, some North American white-tailed deer often stay within thicker stretches of forest. Towering pine trees in some areas offer them protection from falling snow and whipping winds.

White-tailed deer are also able to survive in other habitats. This species exists everywhere from farmlands to deserts to swamps. White-tailed deer do best in environments that feature thickets. Thickets are dense clumps of bushes and trees. These areas provide them with shelter from the weather and a place to hide from predators. It is also important that white-tailed deer are close to the plant life on which they feed. Nearby rivers, lakes, and streams are needed so the deer can drink water.

Thick forests offer deer protection from the elements during winter months.

Physical Features

Adult white-tailed deer range in size from 70 to 300 pounds (32 to 136 kilograms). From head to tail, they stretch 4.6 to 5.6 feet (1.4 to 1.7 meters) on average. Some can grow to be much larger, while some are smaller. Bucks are larger than does.

White-tailed deer have long, slender bodies. Their muscular legs end in narrow hooves. The underside of each deer's short tail is covered in white fur. This physical feature is what gives the species its name.

Bucks are well known for their amazing antlers. The main branches of these antlers can reach up to 30 inches (76 centimeters) in length. However, they rarely exceed 24 inches (61 cm). They feature a series of sharp points called tines. Bucks shed their antlers every winter and grow new ones in the spring.

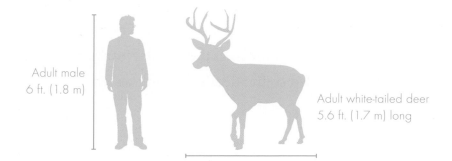

Adult male
6 ft. (1.8 m)

Adult white-tailed deer
5.6 ft. (1.7 m) long

Sometimes antlers take on irregular shapes if they are damaged while growing.

CHAPTER 2

Surviving in the Wild

White-tailed deer have a variety of remarkable features that help them survive in the wild. These characteristics help them escape predators and find food to eat. A white-tailed deer's diet includes buds, leaves, shoots, and lichens. It also includes bark, berries, fruits, grains, nuts, and mushrooms.

Deer are ruminants. This means they have a stomach that is divided into four separate chambers. Food is partly digested—or broken down—in the first two chambers. Bacteria in the stomach help to break down the food. This allows the deer to absorb nutrients. The bacteria also absorb the nutrients the deer need to survive.

To aid the digestive process, deer regurgitate their partially digested food before it leaves the first two chambers. This regurgitated food is called cud. After regurgitating, deer chew up the cud and swallow it again. This allows the food to be further broken down. Their third and fourth stomach chambers complete the digestion process.

White-tailed deer use their back teeth to grind up plants as they chew.

Leaps and Bounds

White-tailed deer rely on speed and agility to escape from danger. Their natural predators include bobcats, mountain lions, wolves, and coyotes. White-tailed deer are able to move at speeds of up to 30 miles (48 kilometers) per hour. In addition, their powerful, muscular legs allow them to leap as high as 10 feet (3 m) into the air. They can also jump across long distances. Scientists estimate that white-tailed deer are capable of covering 30 feet (9 m) in a single bound.

Another physical feature that helps white-tailed deer move fast and efficiently is their hooves. The outer portion of a deer hoof is strong. It absorbs any shock that occurs when a white-tailed deer hits the ground after leaping. The inner part of the hoof is softer. It offers both cushioning and a gripping power called traction. Extra traction prevents white-tailed deer from slipping and sliding as they run.

A white-tailed deer can leap over fences in a single bound.

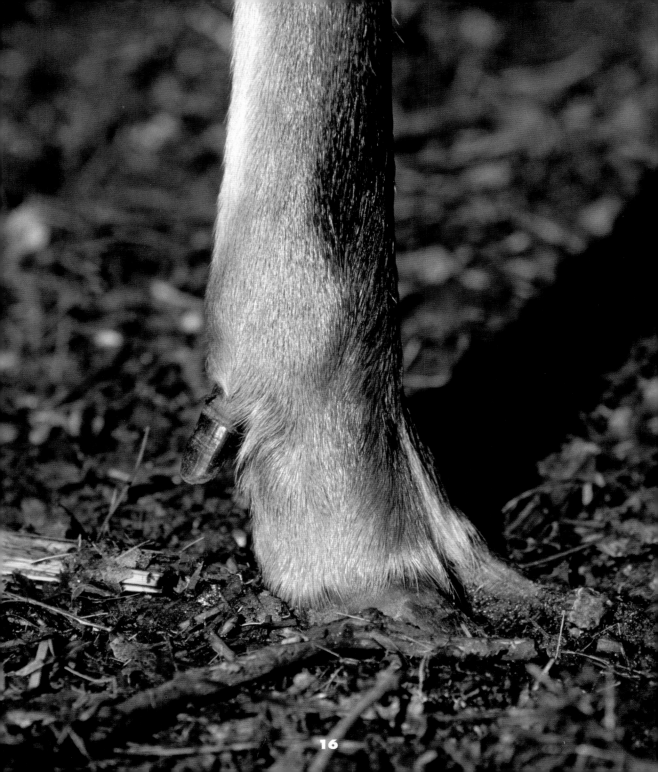

Handy Hooves

White-tailed deer use their hooves for more than just quick movement. They also use their hooves to defend themselves. A white-tailed deer that comes face-to-face with a predator might attack with its front hooves. Such kicks are capable of killing many of the animals that prey on deer.

Scientists believe that certain deer can communicate with their hooves. In addition to grunting and snorting, white-tailed deer often stomp their hooves on the ground when they sense danger is near. This behavior tells enemies to back away. It also causes glands between the two parts of the deer's hoof to release a special scent. Other deer that pass by the area detect this odor. They recognize it as a warning signal.

FUN FACT! White-tailed deer use their hooves to dig for food that is buried under leaves and snow.

A deer's powerful hooves leave behind heart-shaped tracks as the deer walks.

An Overview of Antlers

When a buck begins growing its antlers in spring, they are soft and covered in a protective coat of velvet. By late summer or early fall, the buck has scraped away this velvet by rubbing against tree bark. Some people suspect that the hardened pair of antlers that remains provides extra defense against predators.

White-tailed deer sometimes also scrape their antlers against trees during the fall, when it comes time to mate. This activity leaves behind a smell. This smell attracts does. It also issues a challenge to nearby bucks. Bucks often compete for the right to mate with does. White-tailed bucks depend on their antlers to show their dominance over other males. One of the ways they do this is by locking antlers. Whichever buck backs down first is usually considered the less dominant of the pair.

White-tailed bucks leave behind distinctive markings
as they rub their antlers against trees.

Hidden and Warm

Another physical feature that helps a white-tailed deer survive is its coat. The coloring of a white-tailed deer's hair provides it with natural camouflage. This means that a deer's fur helps it blend in with its surroundings.

In summer months, a reddish-brown coat makes it difficult to spot white-tailed deer among the trees, shrubs, and grasses found in wooded areas and meadows. Scientists believe that a fawn's white spots serve a similar purpose. They camouflage the young deer as it lies hidden and still during the times when its mother is away.

As winter approaches, a white-tailed deer's coat is replaced with thicker fur. This gives the deer's coat a grayish-brown color. A deer's winter hairs are long and hollow. Their size and shape prevent heat from escaping the deer's body. This means the hairs offer protection against falling temperatures.

FUN FACT! Fawns lose their spots when they are about five to six months old.

Fawns lie still in tall grass or other well-hidden areas to stay out of predators' sight.

Incredible Eyes

White-tailed deer have a wide field of vision. This means the area they are able to see when their eyes are fixed in one position is very large. A deer's eyes are located on the sides of its head. This feature allows the animal to take in a broad view of its surroundings at any given moment. It also increases the odds that a white-tailed deer will notice predators as they approach.

Scientists have determined that a deer's eyes are roughly nine times more sensitive to changes in light than a human's eyes are. This helps them graze between dusk and dawn, when the world around them is filled with darkness. By not feeding in broad daylight, white-tailed deer run less risk of being spotted by predators.

However, these deer do not have completely perfect vision. While white-tailed deer can detect even slight motions, they are not very good at seeing colors.

Deer use their eyes to keep a constant lookout for threats, even as they are eating or drinking.

Other Exceptional Senses

White-tailed deer also rely on their other senses to steer clear of danger. A deer's large ears have a cupped shape. This shape is good at picking up quiet sounds and making them loud enough for the deer to hear. A deer's ears are also capable of moving in different directions. This flexibility helps the deer determine the location of a sound.

A white-tailed deer depends on its hearing to both detect and flee from predators. As the deer is running from an enemy, it uses its ears to figure out if it is being chased from behind. At the same time, the animal is also able to focus on any noises ahead of it.

A white-tailed deer has a remarkable sense of smell. Scientists have discovered that a large part of the deer's brain sends and receives signals with the nose. This allows the animal to recognize many different scents. Experts say that white-tailed deer can identify the smell of a predator from up to 600 feet (183 m) away!

When a deer hears something that catches its interest, its large ears quickly perk up.

CHAPTER 3

A Deer's Day-to-Day Life

Most white-tailed deer live an average of 2 to 3 years in wild areas where hunting is allowed. Those that live in areas where hunting is not allowed often reach the age of 10. A few have even survived for up to 20 years within their natural environment. White-tailed deer tend to have a longer life span in captivity. Captive deer can live between 10 and 16 years.

An adult white-tailed doe often lives in a small group that includes her fawns and occasionally other females she gave birth to the previous year. It might also include her mother and sisters. The home range, or area in which this group is found, covers roughly 400 to 1,200 acres (162 to 486 hectares) of habitat. White-tailed bucks typically leave their mother when they are about a year old. After that point, they live alone or in groups made up of two to five other males. Bucks normally travel across a range of 640 to 1,920 acres (259 to 777 ha).

White-tailed deer often travel together in small family groups.

Mating Season

Mating season for white-tailed deer usually lasts from late fall through early winter. During this period, females begin giving off signals that they are ready to mate.

Meanwhile, bucks challenge each other for mates. In addition to locking antlers, they use body language that includes staring and lowering their ears to demonstrate dominance. It is not uncommon for a dominant buck to reproduce with several different does in a single mating season.

A white-tailed deer is pregnant for about seven months after mating. Younger does typically produce only one fawn at a time. Older deer normally carry twins. On rare occasions, they might have triplets. White-tailed deer do not give birth more than once a year. Their fawns are born in late spring or early summer and weigh roughly 4 to 8 pounds (1.8 to 3.6 kg).

FUN FACT! Scientists believe that does often choose bucks with larger antlers when selecting their mates.

Deer antlers make a rattling sound as they crash together during a fight between two bucks.

A Glimpse at Growing Up

Most baby deer are able to walk within an hour of birth. However, they do not venture out much into the world around them at first. Does make sure their fawns stay hidden in the brush for about three weeks. Mother deer leave their young to forage but return four to six times a day to feed them. At first, fawns get their food from **nursing**. Bucks do not remain with the does to help them care for their babies.

As soon as a fawn can keep up with its mother, it begins to follow her as she moves around her home range. The young deer gradually adds plants to its diet. It usually stops nursing when it is 10 to 12 weeks old. Young deer might stay by their mother's side for several months. They can begin mating and having fawns of their own the following mating season after they are born. However, many of them do not begin mating until they are slightly older.

Fawns are highly vulnerable to attacks from predators.

CHAPTER 4

Past and Present Identity

White-tailed deer are part of the **genus** known as *Odocoileus*. The first *Odocoileus* species appeared on Earth between 3.9 million and 3.5 million years ago. Scientists say that *Odocoileus virginianus*, or white-tailed deer, are the oldest species of deer living today.

Early Americans relied heavily on these animals for survival. Both Native Americans and European settlers hunted them for their meat and skins. Later, people began killing the deer for sport. Unfortunately, there were certain periods of time when overhunting occurred. The white-tailed deer population decreased when this happened. In response, government leaders created laws that protect the animals.

There are currently at least 30 million white-tailed deer in North America alone. This includes members of about 38 different **subspecies**. Scientists identify most of these subspecies based on the areas in which they live.

Centuries ago, Native Americans hunted deer by disguising themselves in deer skins.

White-Tailed Subspecies

Virginia white-tailed deer, or southern white-tailed deer, are an example of a widespread subspecies within the United States. Early settlers often wrote about Virginia white-tailed deer in their journals, letters, and business records. People almost drove this subspecies to the point of extinction in the late 1800s and early 1900s. Today, Virginia white-tailed deer are no longer in danger of dying out.

Unfortunately, the same is not true for Key deer. These deer exist on the Florida Keys, which is a chain of islands located off Florida's southern coast. They make up the smallest subspecies of white-tailed deer. Key deer usually weigh no more than 85 pounds (39 kg). Hunting, hurricanes, and especially habitat destruction have led scientists and government officials to declare Key deer endangered. Experts believe only 600 to 800 members of this subspecies currently remain in the wild.

The Key deer subspecies is slowly disappearing.

Comparisons with a Close Relative

The mule deer is the white-tailed deer's closest living relative. The mule deer and the white-tailed deer are the only two species within the genus *Odocoileus*. Yet there are several important differences that separate these animals.

Mule deer mainly live in western North America and northern Mexico. White-tailed deer cover a far wider geographic range. White-tailed deer also tend to be slightly smaller than mule deer. In addition, a mule deer has a black-tipped tail and longer ears than its relative.

Another major difference between mule deer and white-tailed deer is their antlers. A white-tailed deer's antlers feature tines that stretch outward from a single main stem. However, the second tines on each of a mule deer's main antler beams are usually forked.

Mule deer are named for their long ears, which look like mule ears.

CHAPTER 5

Humans and Shared Habitats

White-tailed deer often live very close to humans. This can cause several problems. For example, residents of states with large numbers of white-tailed deer often have to be extra cautious while driving. Accidentally crashing into a deer can cause serious damage to a person's car. It can also result in injury and even death for both the animal and anyone traveling inside the vehicle.

In addition, white-tailed deer have been known to carry ticks. These parasites are capable of spreading diseases to humans and other animals. Some people complain that white-tailed deer destroy private and public property. It is not unusual for this species to be attracted to plant life in yards, farms, gardens, and parks. Too many white-tailed deer can lead to the destruction of these areas.

People use several different methods to control white-tailed deer populations. Sometimes they treat wild deer with medicines to keep them from reproducing. Other efforts include building fences and moving deer to new locations.

In some parts of North America, it is common to spot white-tailed deer in yards or near streets and highways.

Dealing with Deer Problems

Controlled hunting is the main way that authorities work to manage deer populations. Hunters can sign up to purchase tags that give them permission to kill a certain number of deer during hunting seasons. Wildlife authorities ensure that the right number of tags are given out each year. This allows them to keep deer populations in check while preventing overhunting.

Deer hunting also provides wildlife management services with an important source of income. The money that hunters spend on deer tags and other fees associated with hunting goes toward such important causes as protecting endangered species.

People are constantly searching for new ways to balance their own needs with an awareness of the natural world around them. As they learn more about the white-tailed deer, they will search for better ways to live alongside this majestic animal.

Wildlife experts are trying to ensure that white-tailed deer continue to play a healthy role in their environment.

Words to Know

agility (uh-JIL-uh-tee) — the ability to move fast and easily

bacteria (bak-TEER-ee-uh) — microscopic, single-celled living things that exist everywhere and that can either be useful or harmful

bucks (BUHKS) — male deer

captivity (kap-TIV-uh-tee) — the condition of being held or trapped by people

doe (DOH) — a female deer

endangered (en-DAYN-jurd) — at risk of becoming extinct, usually because of human activity

environments (en-VYE-ruhn-muhnts) — the natural surroundings of living things, such as the air, land, or sea

extinction (ik-STINGK-shuhn) — complete disappearance of a species from a certain area or from the entire world

fawn (FAWN) — a deer less than a year old

forage (FOR-ij) — to go in search of food

genus (JEE-nuhs) — a group of related plants or animals that is larger than a species but smaller than a family

glands (GLANDZ) — organs in the body that produce or release natural chemicals

habitats (HAB-uh-tats) — the places where an animal or a plant naturally lives

lichens (LYE-kuhnz) — flat, spongelike growths on rocks, walls, and trees that consist of algae and fungi growing close together

mammals (MAM-uhlz) — warm-blooded animals that have hair or fur and usually give birth to live young

mate (MATE) — to join together to produce babies

nursing (NUR-sing) — feeding a baby milk that is produced by its mother

nutrients (NOO-tree-uhnts) — substances such as proteins, minerals, or vitamins that are needed by people, animals, and plants to stay strong and healthy

parasites (PER-uh-sites) — animals or plants that live on or inside of another animal or plant

predators (PRED-uh-turz) — animals that live by hunting other animals for food

regurgitate (ree-GUR-juh-tate) — to bring food that has been swallowed back up to the mouth

ruminants (ROO-muh-nuhnts) — cud-chewing, hoofed mammals that have a stomach divided into four chambers

species (SPEE-sheez) — one of the groups into which animals and plants of the same genus are divided; members of the same species can mate and have offspring

subspecies (SUHB-spee-sheez) — groups of animals that are part of the same species but are different in some important ways

Habitat Map

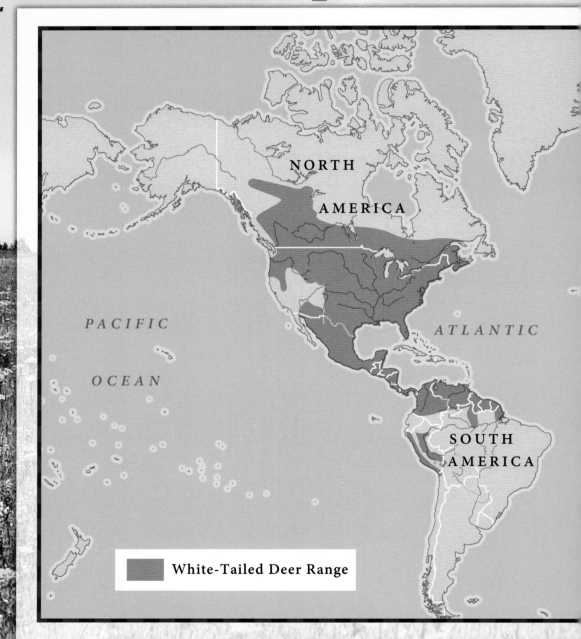

NORTH AMERICA

SOUTH AMERICA

PACIFIC

OCEAN

ATLANTIC

White-Tailed Deer Range

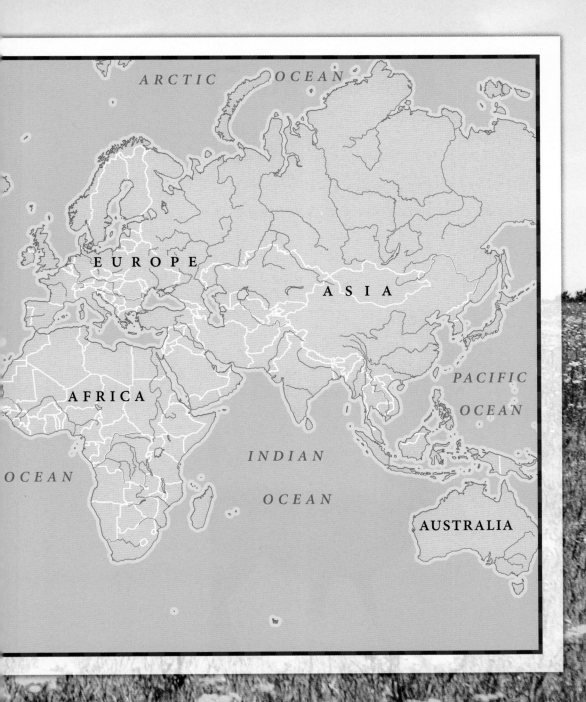

ARCTIC OCEAN

EUROPE

ASIA

AFRICA

PACIFIC
OCEAN

OCEAN

INDIAN

OCEAN

AUSTRALIA

Find Out More

Books

Magby, Meryl. *White-Tailed Deer*. New York: PowerKids Press, 2014.

McGill, Jordan. *Deer*. New York: AV2 by Weigl, 2012.

Webster, Christine. *Deer*. New York: AV2 by Weigl, 2013.

Visit this Scholastic Web site for more information on white-tailed deer:
www.factsfornow.scholastic.com
Enter the keywords **White-Tailed Deer**

Index

Page numbers in *italics* indicate a photograph or map.

About the Author

Katie Marsico is the author of more than 100 children's books. She routinely spots white-tailed deer when she drives past forest preserves near her home in Illinois. Marsico dedicates this book to Shelly Messenger, an amazing and much loved educator.